A01

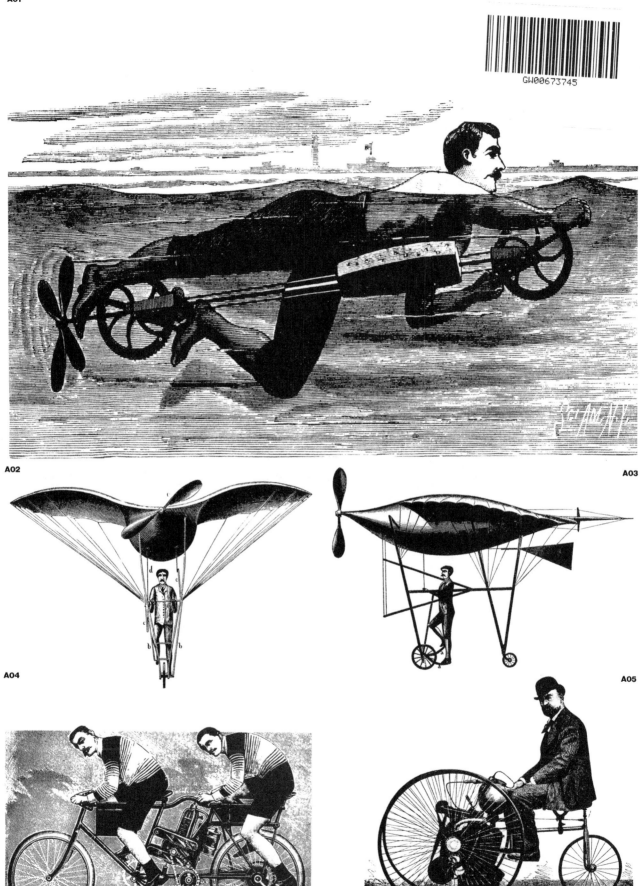

A02

A03

A04

A05

A07

A06

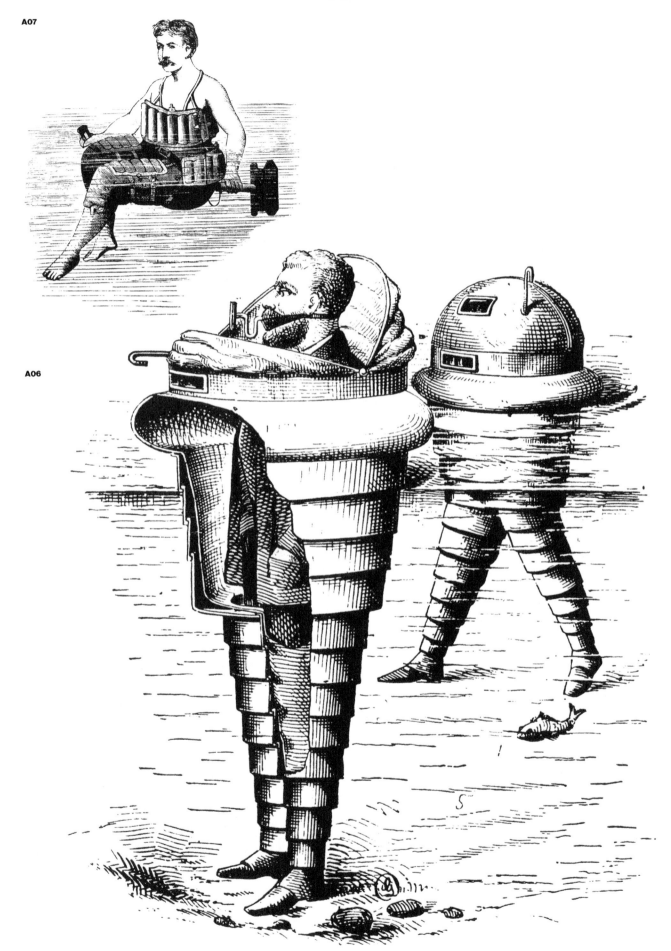

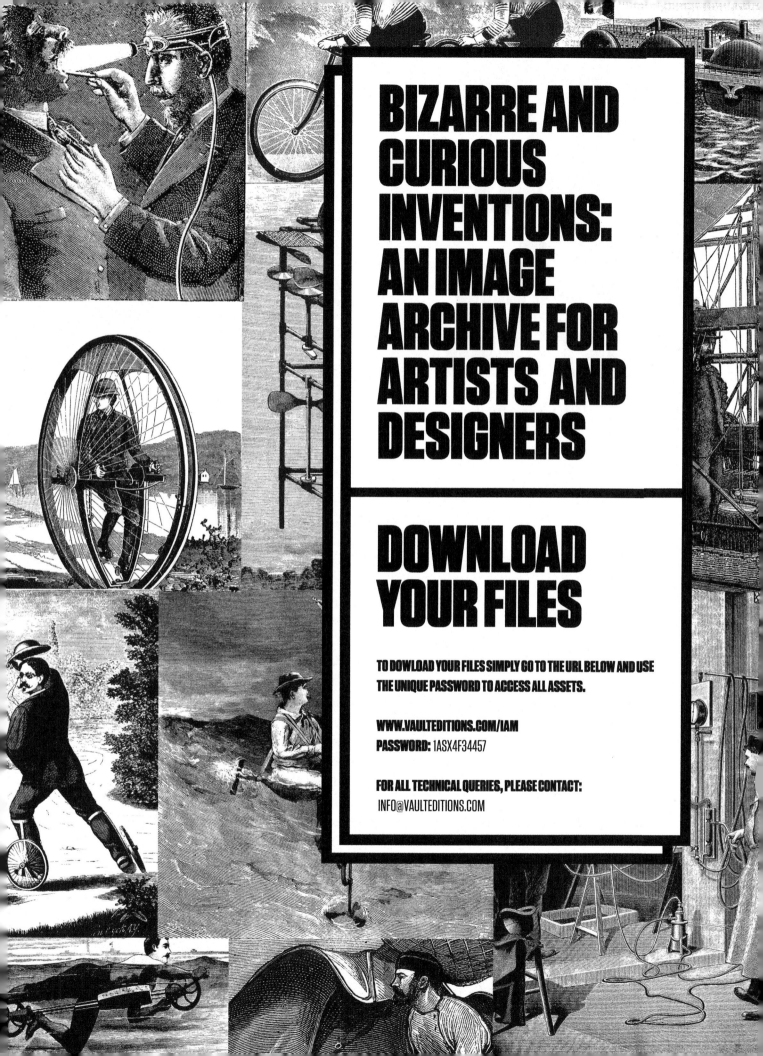

BIZARRE AND CURIOUS INVENTIONS: AN IMAGE ARCHIVE FOR ARTISTS AND DESIGNERS

DOWNLOAD YOUR FILES

TO DOWLOAD YOUR FILES SIMPLY GO TO THE URL BELOW AND USE THE UNIQUE PASSWORD TO ACCESS ALL ASSETS.

WWW.VAULTEDITIONS.COM/IAM

PASSWORD: 1ASX4F34457

FOR ALL TECHNICAL QUERIES, PLEASE CONTACT:
INFO@VAULTEDITIONS.COM

BIZZARE AND CURIOUS INVENTIONS: AN IMAGE ARCHIVE FOR ARTISTS AND DESIGNERS

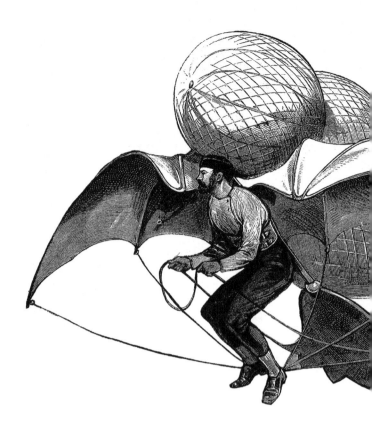

Bizarre and Curious Inventions: A Pictoral Archive for Artists & Designers is a premium collection of hundreds of rare, high quality, digitised engravings and etchings from 18th and 19th century sources for use in personal or commercial creative projects.

This is an essential reference for graphic designers, illustrators, collage artists and students wanting to speed up their workflow, expand their collection of creative resources and take their work to the next level.

Our titles are suitable for artists of all disciplines and skill levels, from industry professionals to art and design students or for curious readers.

This archive is an amazing resource designed to help and inspire artists. By collaging multiple images together, you can create limitless impressive and dynamic designs in minutes that will impress everyone, no matter what your skill level is. Get a competitive advantage over your peers and start creating amazing artwork today. We have carefully restored the artwork and provided a download link within the publication where you can download high-resolution files in JPEG and TIFF files with backgrounds removed to speed up your workflow.

Vault Editions' team of designers and illustrators have spent a lifetime hunting and restoring vintage woodcuts and engravings from around the world to create amazing artwork with. Now, we are opening the vault of our archives to the public. Within this collection, you will find rare, high-quality images carefully curated by our team of professional artists and designers to help you to create book cover designs, gig-posters, logos, t-shirt designs, invitations, packaging, album artwork, editorial illustrations, and more.

ISBN: 978-1-925968-00-2

Bibliographical Note

This book is a new work created by Avenue House Press Pty Ltd.

A21

A22

A24

A23

A25

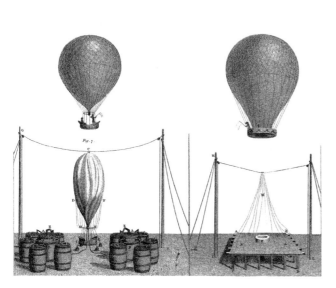

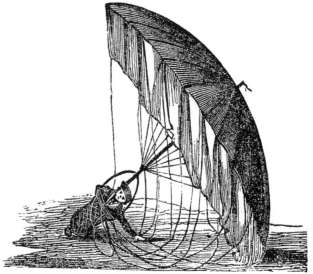

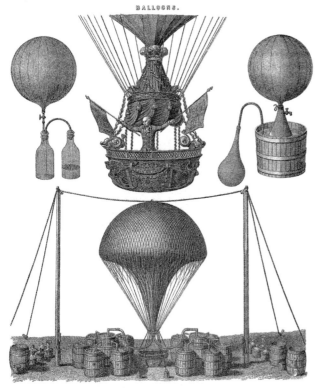

BIZZARE & CURIOUS INVENTIONS

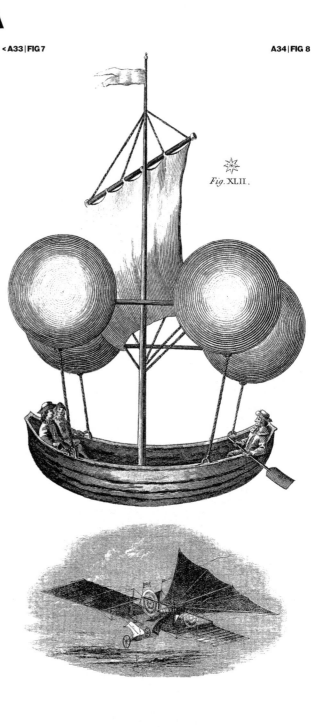

Fig. XLII.

A35 | FIG 9

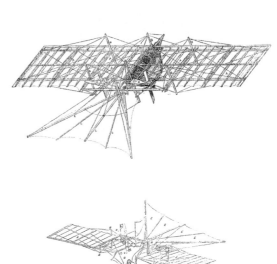

A36 | FIG 10

BIZZARE & CURIOUS INVENTIONS

A38 | FIG 12

A39

AERONAUTICS.

Plate I.

Lana's Aeronautic Machine

Montgolfier's Balloon

Blanchard's Balloon

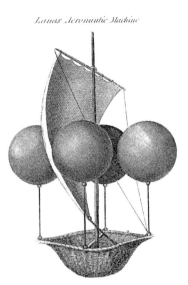

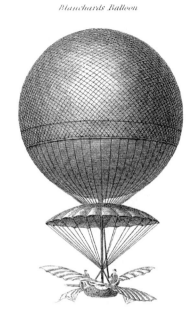

Garnerin Ascending

Charles & Roberts' Balloon

Garnerin Descending

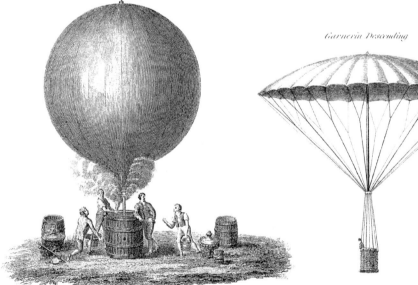

Fig. 7

Form of the Wings employed by Lanatoli

form of the Wings employed by Blanchard

Drawn by Joseph Clement.

Published as the Act directs April 1818 by Rest Fenner, Paternoster Row.

Engraved by A.W.Warren & Son.

A41

B. ARNAUD

LYON & PARIS

A42

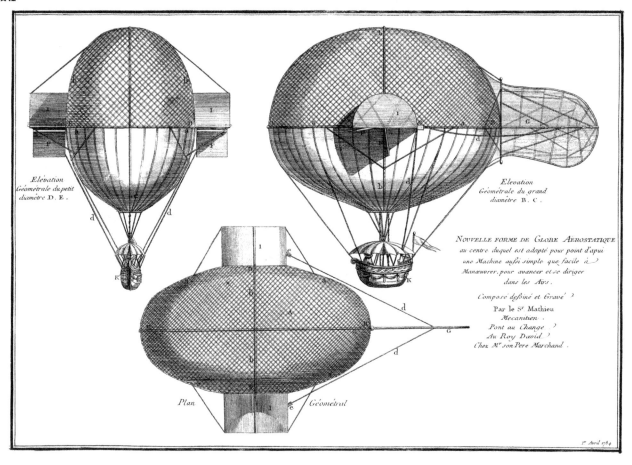

Elevation
Géométrale du petit
diamètre D. E.

Elevation
Géométrale du grand
diamètre B. C.

NOUVELLE FORME DE GLOBE AEROSTATIQUE
au centre duquel est adapté pour point d'apui
une Machine aussi simple que facile à
Manœuvrer, pour avancer et se diriger
dans les Airs.

Composé dessiné et Gravé
Par le S.r Mathieu
Mecanitien.
Pont au Change
Au Roy David
Chez M.r son Pere Marchand.

Plan   Géométral

1.er Avril 1784

BIZZARE & CURIOUS INVENTIONS

B03

B04

B05

B

B06

B07

BIZZARE & CURIOUS INVENTIONS

B08

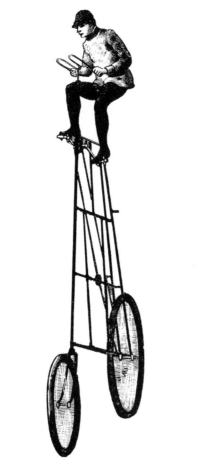

B09

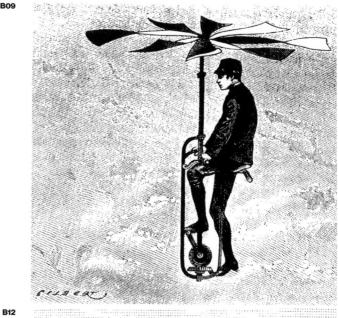

B10

B12

B11

B13

B14

B15

B16

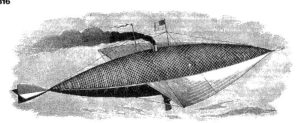

B17

B19

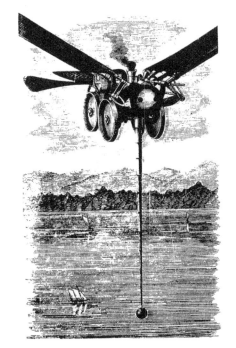

B18

B20 | FIG 13

BIZZARE & CURIOUS INVENTIONS

B

B23 | FIG 15

B24 | FIG 15

B25 | FIG 16

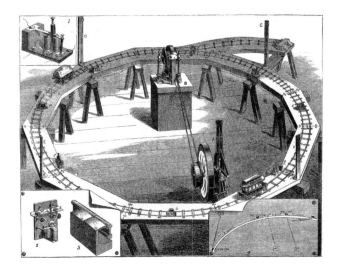

B01 | **FIG 17**

B01 | **FIG 19**

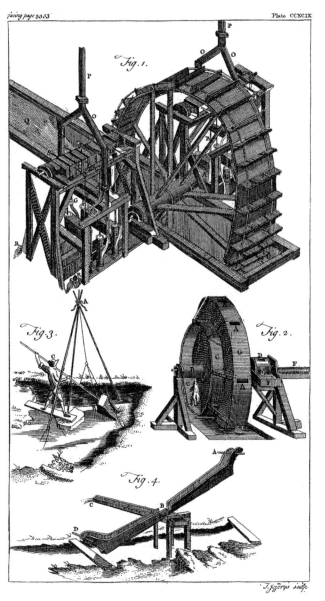

BIZZARE & CURIOUS INVENTIONS

BIZZARE & CURIOUS INVENTIONS

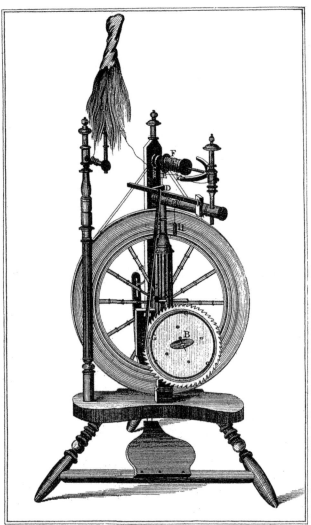

B28 | **FIG 18**

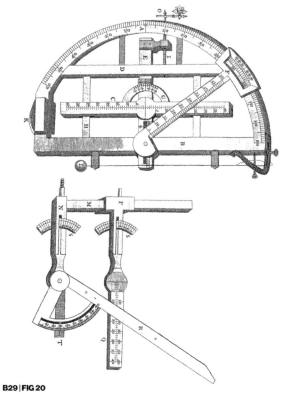

B29 | **FIG 20**

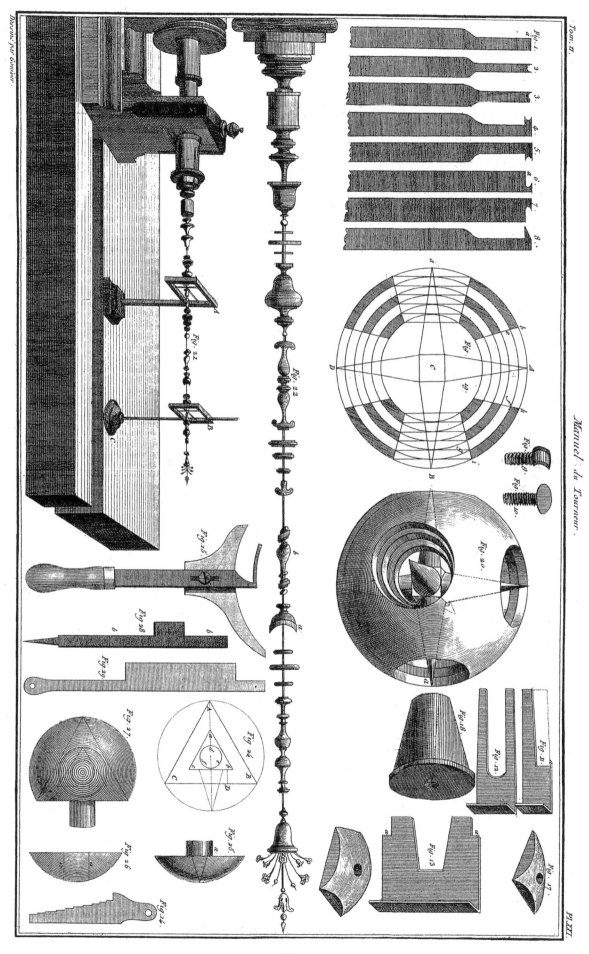

C01

C02

C03

C04

C05

C06

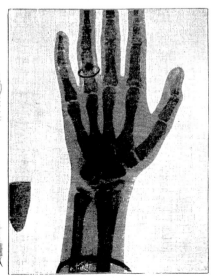

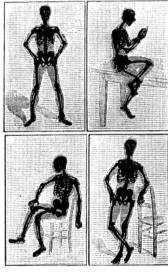

C

C07

C09   **C08**

C10

C11

C

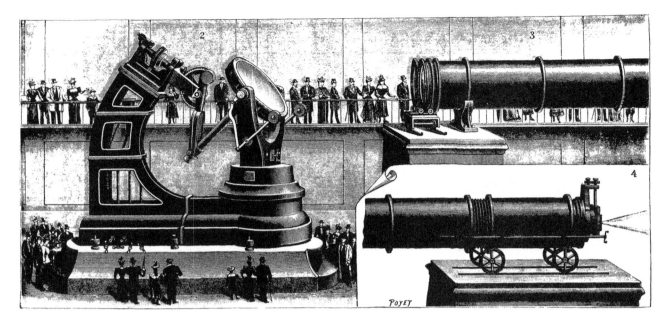

C12

C13

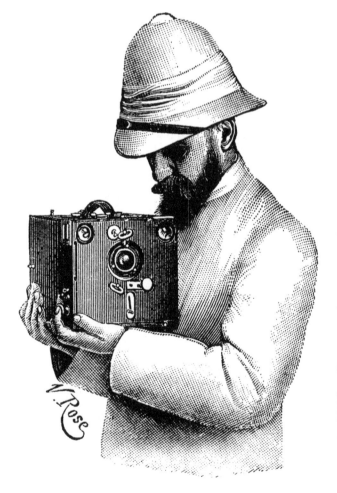

C14

C15

C17

C16

D

D01

BIZZARE & CURIOUS INVENTIONS

D02

D03

D04

D09

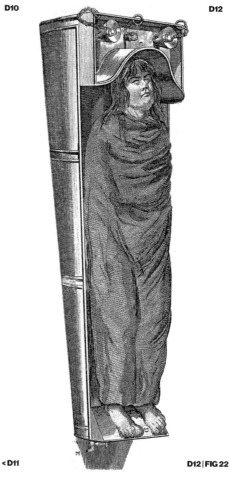

D10

D12

< D11

D12 | FIG 22

F01

F02

F03

F05

F04

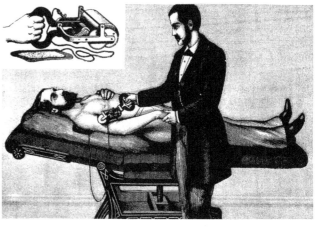

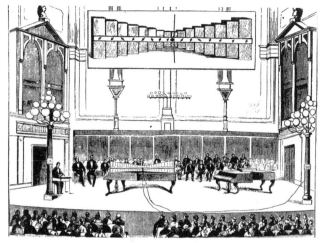

F06

F07

F08

F09

<F10

F12 >

<F11

F

BIZZARE & CURIOUS INVENTIONS

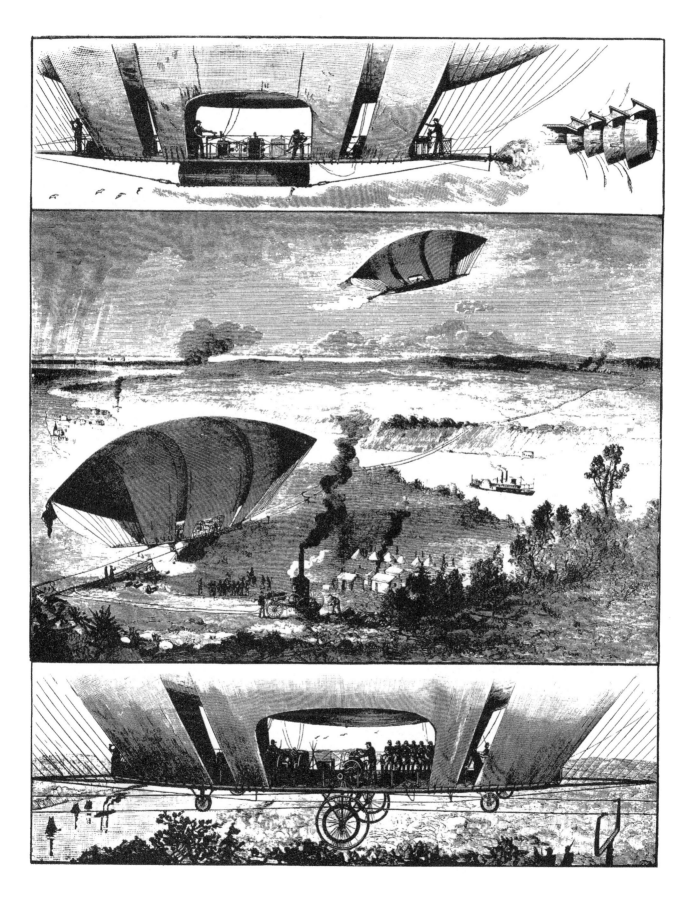

F15

F16

F17

F18 >

F19

F20

F21

G01

G02

G03

G04

G05

G06

G07

G08

G09

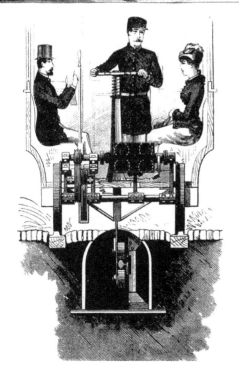

G11

G10

G12

G13

G14

45

G

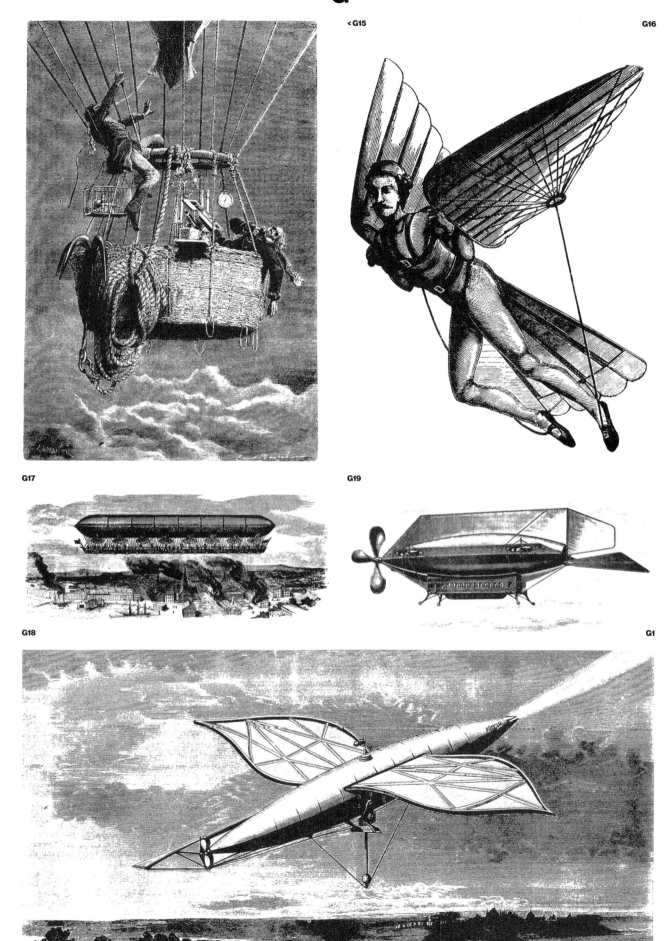

G20

G21

G22

G23

BRIDGE.

Blackfriars Bridge.

London Bridge

Waterloo Bridge.

Southwark Iron Bridge.

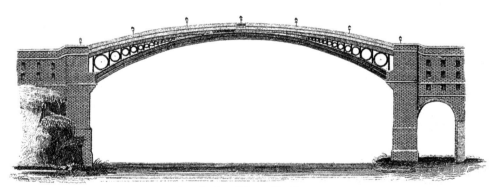

Sunderland Iron Bridge.

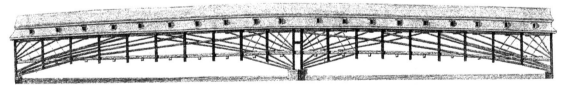

Wooden Bridge over the Rhine at Schaffhausen.

Senatorian Bridge at Rome (restored.)

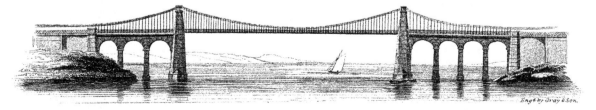

Engd by Gray & Son.

VII.   Taf. 60.   E. 6.

H02 | FIG 27

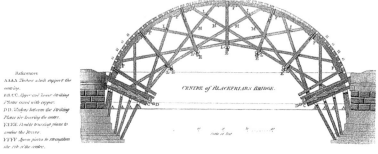

SECTION of an ARCH of WATERLOO BRIDGE with the CENTRE.

H03 | FIG 28

London, Published by Thos Kelly, 17 Paternoster Row, Jan 2, 1848.

H

Pl. XXXVII

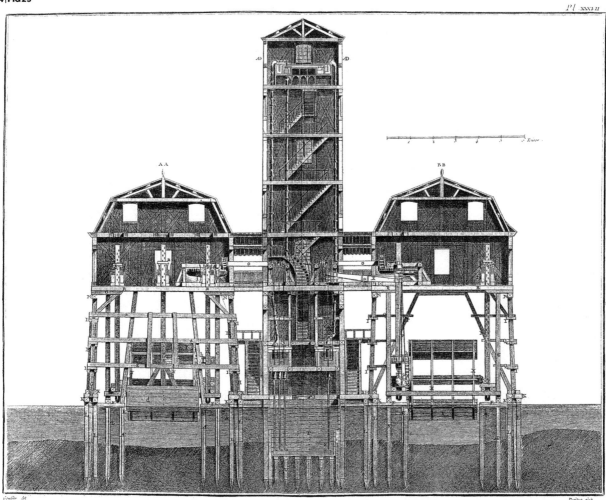

Charpente, Pompe du Pont Notre Dame .

BRIDGE OVER THE NIEMEN AT KOWNO ON WILNA AND DUNABURG LINE, RUSSIA.

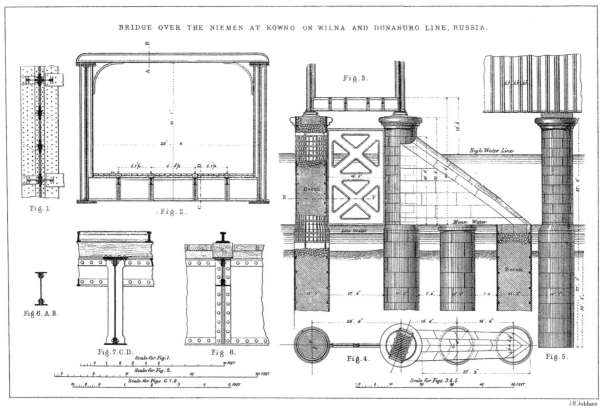

J.R. Jobbins

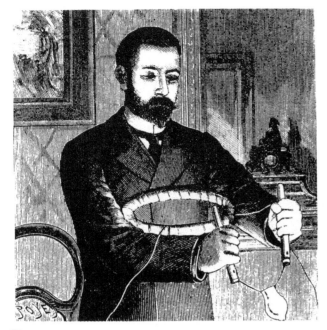

101

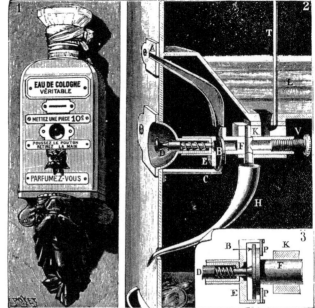

102

103

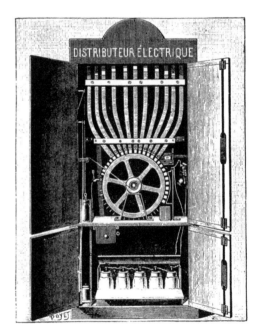

104

106

107

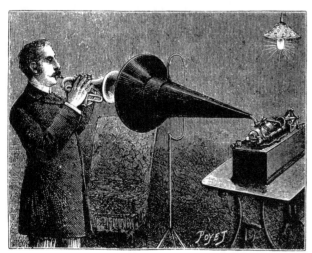

107

109

POYET

108

110

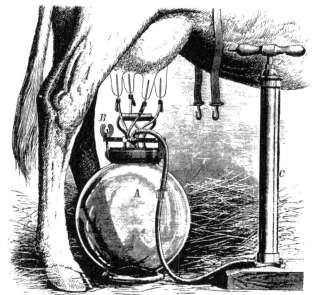

H1

H5 >

H3 >

< H4

H2

116

117

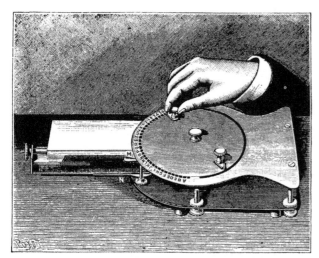

118

119

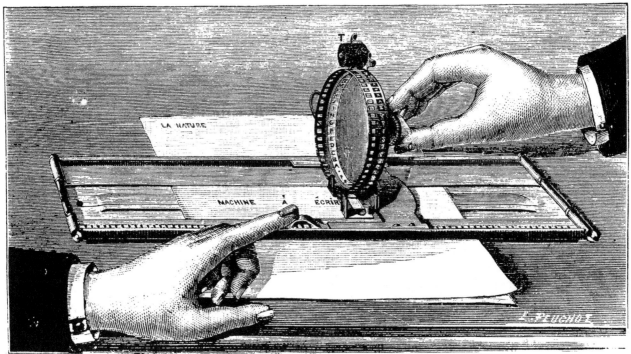

120

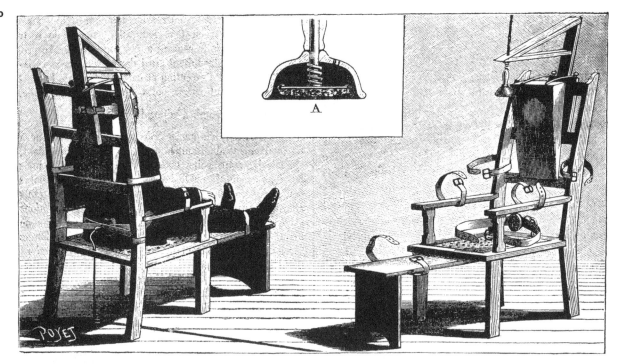

121

J01

J02 >

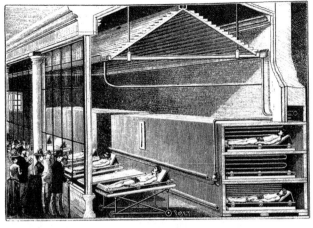

< J03

J04

PUBLICITE PAR LA VÉL

2ᵉ SALON DU CYCLE · PALAIS

J05

< J06

J07

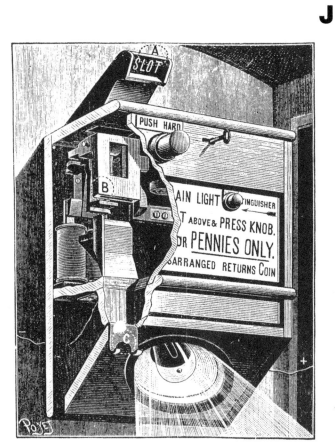

J08

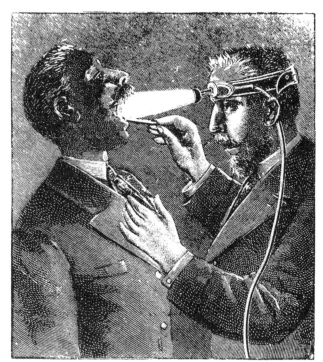

J09

J11

J10

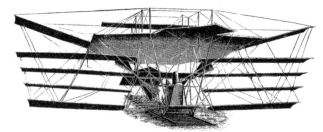

J12

The Beach Hydraulic Tunnelling Shield

J13

.H4

J15

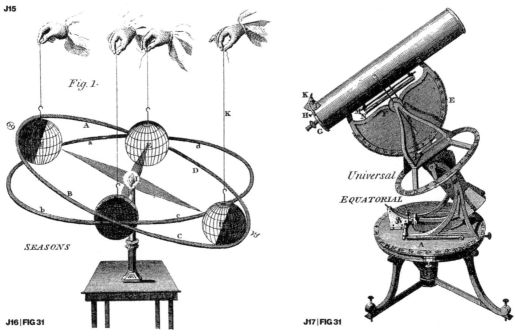

Fig. 1.

SEASONS

J16 | FIG 31

Universal

EQUATORIAL

J17 | FIG 31

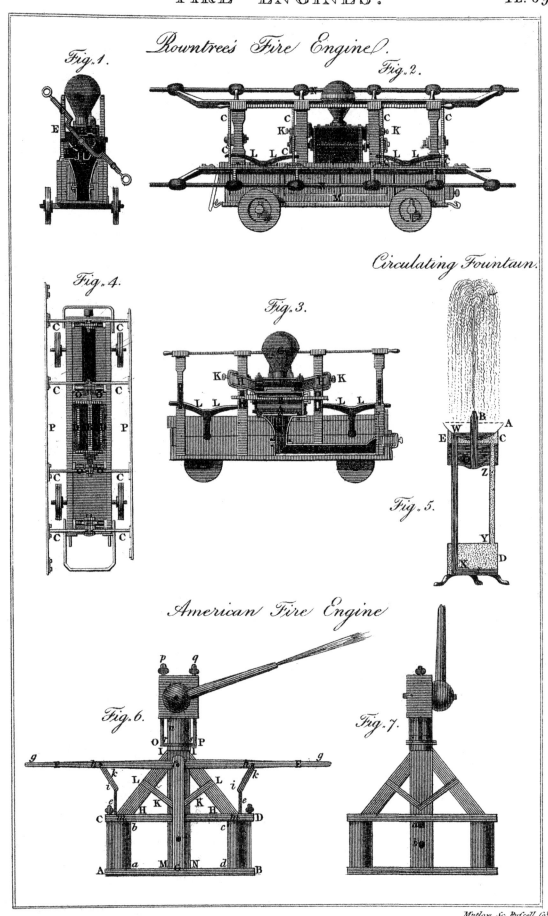

Rowntree's Fire Engine.

Fig. 1.

Fig. 2.

Circulating Fountain.

Fig. 4.

Fig. 3.

Fig. 5.

American Fire Engine

Fig. 6.

Fig. 7.

Mutlow Sc. Rufsell, Co.

K

PLATE 2.

FIRE-ENGINES.

Fig. 1.

Fig. 2.

SMALL HAND FIRE-ENGINE.

STEAM FIRE-ENGINE.

Fig. 3.

Deck

FLOATING STEAM FIRE-ENGINE—Perspective Elevation.

BIZZARE & CURIOUS INVENTIONS

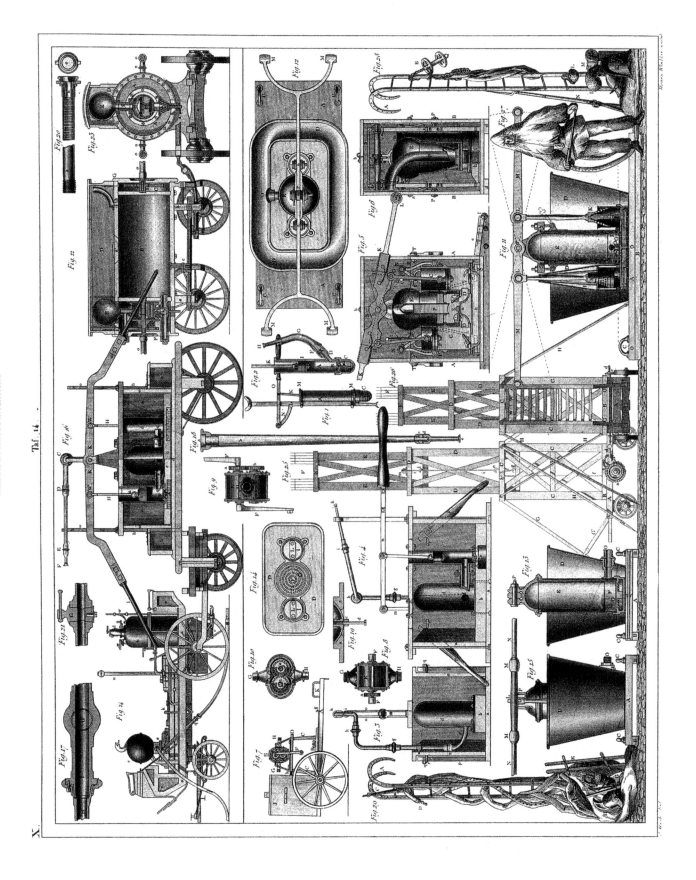

K

K06 | FIG 36

K07 | FIG 37   K08 >

K

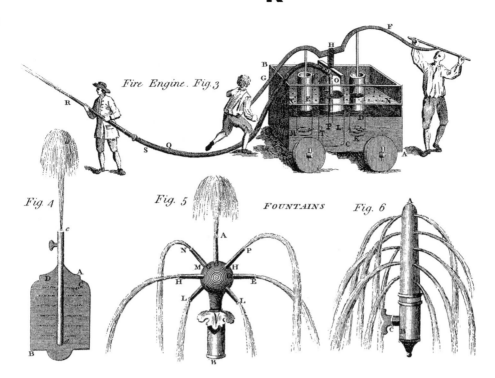

Fire Engine. Fig. 3

Fig. 4   *Fig. 5*   FOUNTAINS   *Fig. 6*

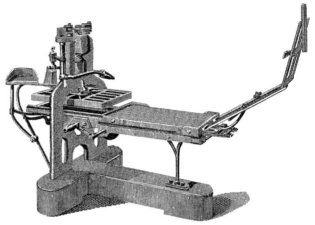

BIZZARE & CURIOUS INVENTIONS

L03 | FIG 40

L

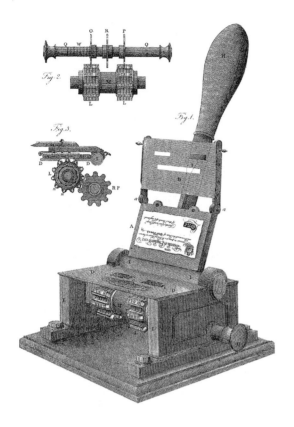

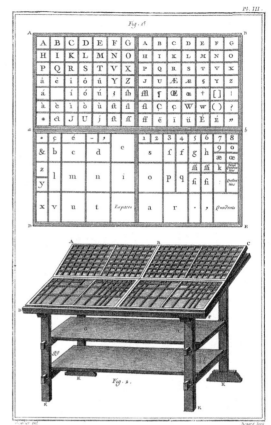

Imprimerie, Casse

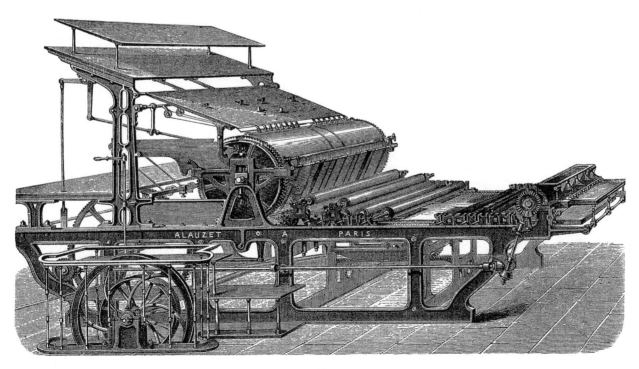

L07 | FIG 44

L08

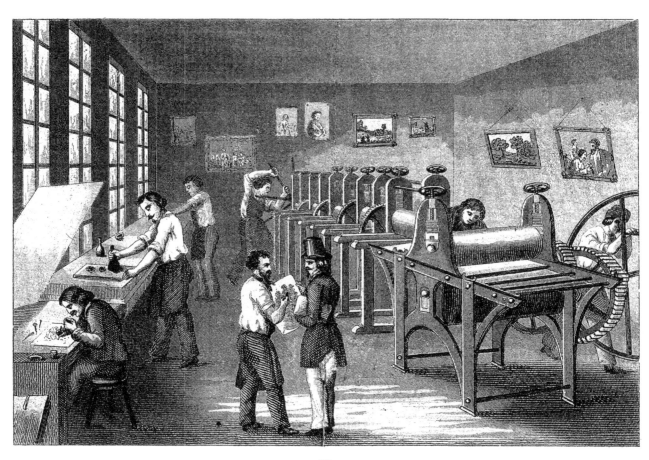

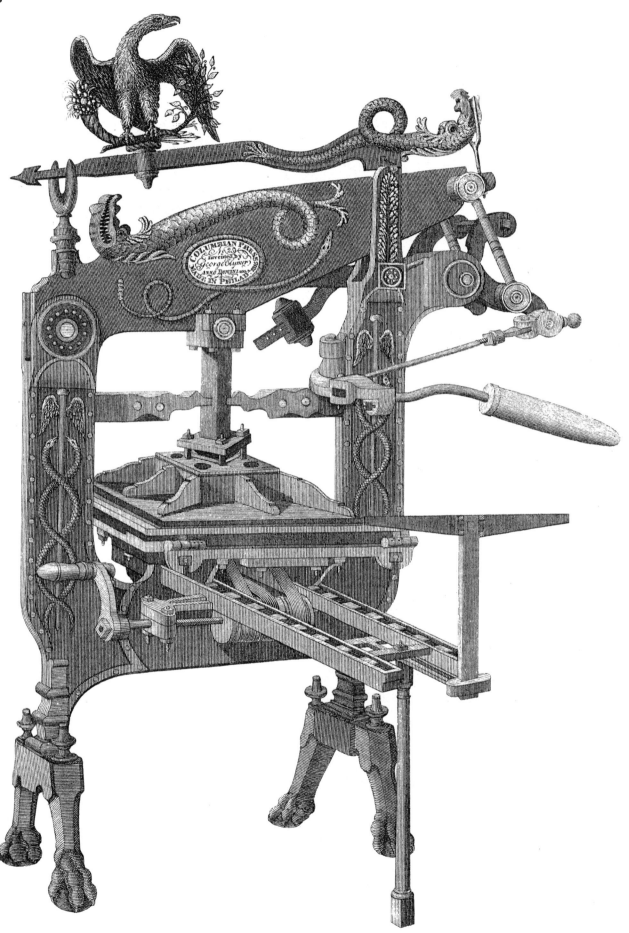

Fig 1: The technicalities of ballooning are being tested. Credit: Wellcome Collection. CC BY. Edited for graphic use by Avenue House Press Pty Ltd, 2019.

Fig2: A man flying in the air with wings and balloons attached to him. Coloured wood engraving. Credit: Wellcome Collection. CC BY. Edited for graphic use by Avenue House Press Pty Ltd, 2019.

Fig 3: A man is standing in the basket of a balloon waving two flags. Engraving. Credit: Wellcome Collection. CC BY. Edited for graphic use by Avenue House Press Pty Ltd, 2019.

Fig 4: A line of hot-air balloons travel over a line of sailing ships. Wood engraving. Credit: Wellcome Collection. CC BY. Edited for graphic use by Avenue House Press Pty Ltd, 2019.

Fig 5: A man with a hot-air balloon device strapped to him. Engraving by Rothwell after De Bruyn. Credit: Wellcome Collection. CC BY. Edited for graphic use by Avenue House Press Pty Ltd, 2019.

Fig 6: A man on horseback suspended from a hot-air balloon. Lithograph after Gustave Janet. Credit: Wellcome Collection. CC BY. Edited for graphic use by Avenue House Press Pty Ltd, 2019.

Fig 7: The basket of a hot-air balloon with two men inside, and an engine with propellors. Process print after E.A Tillyson. Credit: Wellcome Collection. CC BY. Edited for graphic use by Avenue House Press Pty Ltd, 2019.

Fig 8: Three figures in a boat with sails and balloons attached to it. Engraving. Credit: Wellcome Collection. CC BY. Edited for graphic use by Avenue House Press Pty Ltd, 2019.

Fig 9: Men with various flying contraptions strapped to them. Engraving. Credit: Wellcome Collection.CC BY. Edited for graphic use by Avenue House Press Pty Ltd, 2019.

Fig 10: A flying contraption with large wings travels over the water. Wood engraving, 1843. Credit: Wellcome Collection. CC BY. Edited for graphic use by Avenue House Press Pty Ltd, 2019.

Fig 11: Flying machines with propellers in the air. Wood engraving. Credit: Wellcome Collection. CC BY. Edited for graphic use by Avenue House Press Pty Ltd, 2019.

Fig 12: A man is flying in a frame with wings attached and covering him. Wood engraving. Credit: Wellcome Collection. CC BY. Edited for graphic use by Avenue House Press Pty Ltd, 2019.

Fig 13: Respiration d'un air suroxygene, dilate par la diminution de pression (Breathing air suroxygen). Credit: Wellcome Collection. CC BY. Edited for graphic use by Avenue House Press Pty Ltd, 2019.

Fig 14: Machinery: a steam-hammer and operatives. Wood engraving, c.1870 (?). Credit: Wellcome Collection. CC BY. Edited for graphic use by Avenue House Press Pty Ltd, 2019.

Fig 15: Telegraphy: four different inventors' telegraph machines [on exhibition in Paris?]. Wood engraving, (1889?) by Poyet. Credit: Wellcome Collection. CC BY. Edited for graphic use by Avenue House Press Pty Ltd, 2019.

Fig 16: Acoustics: an electrically-powered [?] Edison-type phonograph demonstrated at an exhibition [in Paris?]. Wood engraving. Credit: Wellcome Collection. CC BY. Edited for graphic use by Avenue House Press Pty Ltd, 2019.

Fig 17: A model railway with technical equipment for testing. Wood engraving by T.P. Collings. Credit: Wellcome Collection. CC BY. Edited for graphic use by Avenue House Press Pty Ltd, 2019.

Fig 18: Textiles: a cotton spinning wheel. Engraving by Eastgate. Credit: Wellcome Collection. CC BY. Edited for graphic use by Avenue House Press Pty Ltd, 2019.

Fig 19: Inventions: various items including a fountain-pen, a pendulum, and a pantograph. Engraving by T. Jeffrys. Credit: Wellcome Collection. CC BY. Edited for graphic use by Avenue House Press Pty Ltd, 2019.

Fig 20: Agriculture: a device for estimating the bulk of standing timber. Engraving, 1768. Credit: Wellcome Collection. CC BY. Edited for graphic use by Avenue House Press Pty Ltd, 2019.

Fig 21: A turner's workshop, a man working the crank of a large lathe, the tools ranged around the walls. Engraving by R. Bénard after Lucotte. Credit: Wellcome Collection. CC BY. Edited for graphic use by Avenue House Press Pty Ltd, 2019.

Fig 22: A body covered with a blanket lying on a heated bath for the purpose of resuscitation. Etching, 1790. Credit: Wellcome Collection. CC BY. Edited for graphic use by Avenue House Press Pty Ltd, 2019.

Fig 23: The car of Saint Rosalia. Lithograph, 1823. Credit: Wellcome Collection. CC BY. Edited for graphic use by Avenue House Press Pty Ltd, 2019.

Fig 24: The funeral car of Napoleon Bonaparte. Wood engraving. Cred-

it: Wellcome Collection. CC BY. Edited for graphic use by Avenue House Press Pty Ltd, 2019.

Fig 25: The funeral car of the Duke of Wellington. Wood engraving. Credit: Wellcome Collection. CC BY. Edited for graphic use by Avenue House Press Pty Ltd, 2019.

Fig 26: Civil engineering: various bridges in Britain and Europe. Engraving by Gray and son. Credit: Wellcome Collection. CC BY. Edited for graphic use by Avenue House Press Pty Ltd, 2019.

Fig 27: Civil engineering: various bridges, ancient and modern, around Europe, the Ponte Vecchio, Venice, in the centre. Engraving by A. Krausse. Credit: Wellcome Collection. CC BY. Edited for graphic use by Avenue House Press Pty Ltd, 2019.

Fig 28: Civil engineering: wooden centring for Blackfriars Bridge (above), Waterloo Bridge (below). Engraving by R. Roffe, 1848. Credit: Wellcome Collection. CC BY. Edited for graphic use by Avenue House Press Pty Ltd, 2019.

Fig 29: Carpentry: the pump on Notre Dame bridge, section. Engraving by Defehrt after Goussier. Credit: Wellcome Collection. CC BY. Edited for graphic use by Avenue House Press Pty Ltd, 2019.

Fig 30: Civil engineering: railway bridges at Kaunas. Lithograph by J. R. Jobbins after F. H. Horne. Credit: Wellcome Collection. CC BY. Edited for graphic use by Avenue House Press Pty Ltd, 2019.

Fig 31: The use of instruments and appliances. Engraving. Credit: Wellcome Collection. CC BY. Edited for graphic use by Avenue House Press Pty Ltd, 2019.

Fig 32: Types of fire engine. Etching by Mutlow and Russell, 1809. Credit: Wellcome Collection. CC BY. Edited for graphic use by Avenue House Press Pty Ltd, 2019.

Fig 33: Depictions of fire-engines. Engraving. Credit: Wellcome Collection. CC BY. Edited for graphic use by Avenue House Press Pty Ltd, 2019.

Fig 34: Types of fire-engines and different parts thereof with figure numbers. Engraving by Henry Winkles after G. Heck. Credit: Wellcome Collection. CC BY. Edited for graphic use by Avenue House Press Pty Ltd, 2019.

Fig 35: An extendable ladder is used by fireman to rescue people from fire in the upstairs rooms of a building. Wood engraving. Credit: Wellcome Collection. CC BY

Fig 36: As a fire rages in a house people are being helped to escape by means of chutes extended from the windows to the ground. Etching. Credit: Wellcome Collection. CC BY. Edited for graphic use by Avenue House Press Pty Ltd, 2019.

Fig 37: The use of instruments and appliances. Engraving. Credit: Wellcome Collection. CC BY. Edited for graphic use by Avenue House Press Pty Ltd, 2019.

Fig 38: Printing: section and three-quarter view of the Bramah numerator press for banknote production. Engraving by J. Moffat after J. Farey. Credit: Wellcome Collection. CC BY. Edited for graphic use by Avenue House Press Pty Ltd, 2019.

Fig 39: Printing: a three-quarter view of a press, with a composing stick beneath. Engraving, 1813. Credit: Wellcome Collection. CC BY. Edited for graphic use by Avenue House Press Pty Ltd, 2019.

Fig 40: Textiles: a pair of large presses for block printing calico. Engraving by J. Carter after T. Allom, 1834. Credit: Wellcome Collection. CC BY. Edited for graphic use by Avenue House Press Pty Ltd, 2019.

Fig 41: Printing: three-quarter view and details of the Bramah numerator press for banknote production. Engraving by Mutlow and Russell after J. Farey. Credit: Wellcome Collection. CC BY. Edited for graphic use by Avenue House Press Pty Ltd, 2019.

Fig 42: Plan (top), and three-quarter view (below), of a type case, lettered for a key. Engraving by Benard after L.-J. Goussier. Credit: Wellcome Collection. CC BY. Edited for graphic use by Avenue House Press Pty Ltd, 2019.

Fig 43: A large belt-driven printing machine, made by Alauzet of Paris. Wood engraving. Credit: Wellcome Collection. CC BY. Edited for graphic use by Avenue House Press Pty Ltd, 2019.

Fig 44: A large and busy composing-room at a Parisian [?] printers' establishment. Wood engraving by Trichon Monvoisin [F. A. Trichon] after P. Blanchard. Credit: Wellcome Collection. CC BY. Edited for graphic use by Avenue House Press Pty Ltd, 2019.

Fig 45: A printer's premises, with men engraving, inking plates, and operating presses, examples of their work hang on the walls. Engraving. Credit: Wellcome Collection. CC BY. Edited for graphic use by Avenue House Press Pty Ltd, 2019.

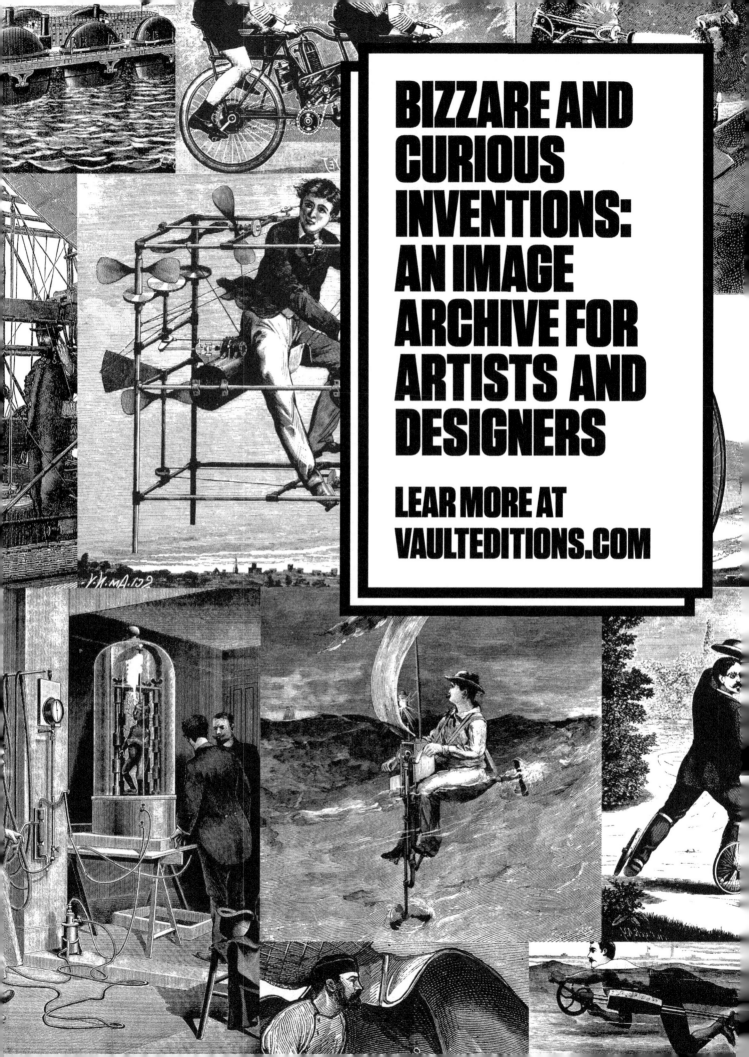

BIZZARE AND CURIOUS INVENTIONS: AN IMAGE ARCHIVE FOR ARTISTS AND DESIGNERS

LEAR MORE AT
VAULTEDITIONS.COM

Printed in Great Britain
by Amazon